MEL BAY'S
EASIEST
DRUM SET
BOOK

By James Morton

1 2 3 4 5 6 7 8 9 0

© 1990 by Mel Bay Publications, Inc., Pacific, MO.
International copyright secured. All rights reserved. Printed in U.S.A.

Contents

Introduction

If you are new to drumming, and to music in general, this book was written for you. If you have played another instrument before, you will probably find the lessons in this book easier to apply. Basic drumming concepts are introduced progressively, so that if you stick with it, you will have a good foundation upon which to further build your musicianship.

Graphic Guides

At the beginning of each lesson, there are graphic displays that are intended to clarify your understanding of the lesson. In the upper right corner of the first page of each lesson is a boxed list of objectives for that lesson, like this:

> **Quarter Note and Rest**
> **Half Note and Rest**
> **Whole Note and Rest**

Above that, there is a small drawing of a standard five-piece drum set, shown from above, like this:

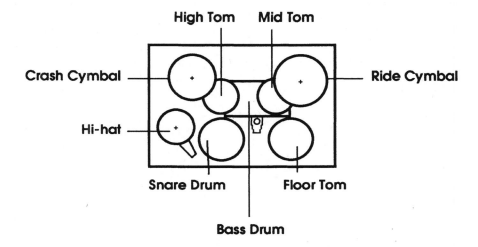

The parts of the drum set which are to be used during that lesson will be shaded, like so:

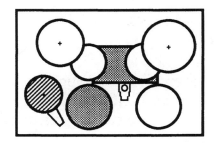

Being a Drummer: A Job Description

WANT ADS

ACCOUNTANT needed to count sheep for wealthy insomniac. Will train. Call 555-6543.

BANK TELLER needed immediately. Must be able to add and subtract. Contact Mr. Cash at 555-4663.

BOY WONDER, must be brave enough to aid middle-aged cartoon hero in fighting crime. Write Mr. Grayson c/o this paper.

COOK wanted for donut shop. Should know the geometric principle of concentric circles. Call Mrs. Caloree at 555-0001.

DRUMMER wanted for rock band. Must keep good time, know when to play fills, and solo when necessary. Should be able to get along with other musicians. Should have own equipment and transportation. Call Joe Guitar at 555-4567.

EXOTIC DANCER, must have good sense of rhythm and no sense of shame. Auditions at The Lonely Sailors' Hangout, 1234 Main St.

PSYCHOLOGIST for counseling center. Clients include: musicians, lonely sailors, and exotic dancers. Send resume´ to Dr. Alan Bates, P.O. Box 99.

There are lots of jobs in the world, and all of them come with job descriptions. A job description lists the duties that a particular job entails. Well, you would be surprised at the number of students who have not thought about what a drummer actually does. Most of us have seen a drummer that particularly inspired us, and that is what made us want to become drummers ourselves. But I do think it is helpful if we clearly list the skills necessary for a drummer to perform adequately. Knowing what you are aiming for will help you focus on the following lessons.

The Role of the Drummer

The role of the drummer can be broken down into three basic functions:

1. To rhythmically contribute to the flow of the music and offer rhythmic support to the other instruments. (In other words — keep the beat!)

2. To embellish the music with appropriate fills, breaks, and punches.

3. To solo when necessary.

These are the primary functions of a drummer. Here are two more that are a little more aesthetic:

4. To conceptualize the musical piece as a whole, being aware of its form and parts.

5. To listen to the other musicians carefully and respond appropriately.

I should point out that the above duties describe the role of any drummer, not just a rock drummer. Anyway, I hope this description clears up any misconceptions you may have had about being a drummer.

Now let's get going!

How to Hold the Sticks

Most rock drummers use what is called the "matched grip" (the left-hand grip is the same as the right-hand grip; they are "matched"). Pick the drumstick up and hold it between the thumb and the first joint of the first finger. Now curve the other three fingers around the stick. Hold the stick securely, but not too tightly.

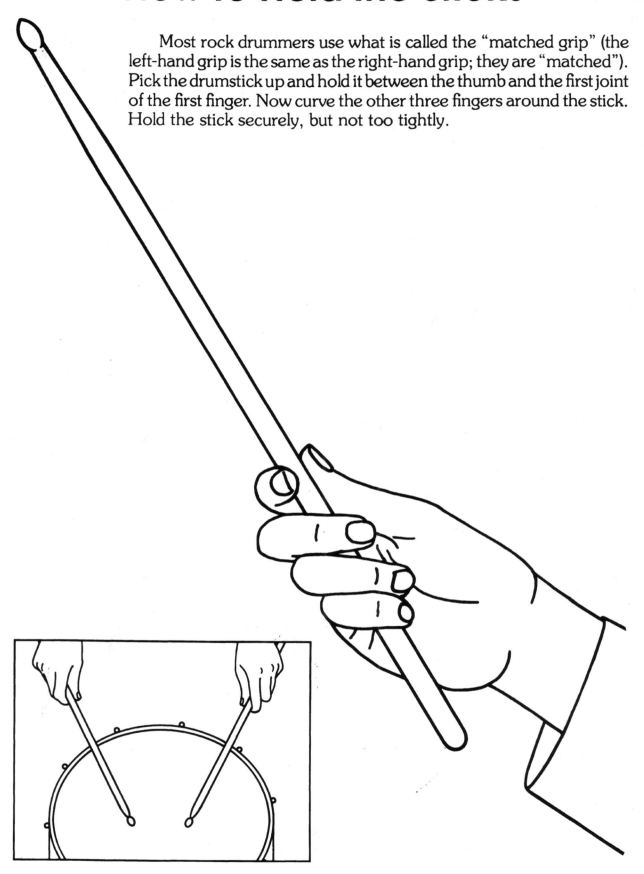

Lesson 1:
Some Basics

Basic Terms

Every kind of music, from a marching band to the latest rock band, is made up of three elements: **melody, harmony,** and **rhythm.** Since a drummer adds rhythmic support to music, his or her primary concern and contribution is **rhythm.** Rhythm is the first element of music.

If you have ever tapped your foot or clapped along with a song, you were feeling the **beat,** or underlying pulse of the music. In writing music, one way of indicating beats is by using a note like this:

This particular note is called the **quarter note,** and it is the note most often thought of as **one beat.** Therefore, when you see a quarter note, you will strike the drum **once.**

Other words to know:

Stroke: A single, completed movement of the stick to the drum by the wrist.

Sticking: The determination of which stick to use for each note. Sticking is indicated by the letters **R** and **L** (for guess what).

Staff: Most music is written on a group of five parallel lines called a **staff.** Note that there are four spaces between the five lines. Traditionally, music for the snare drum is placed on the third space of the staff:

Snare Drum →

As we progress through the following lessons, we will see how other parts of the drum set are notated.

Sticking Patterns

The following sticking patterns are basic to drumming, and they must be mastered and practiced regularly so they can be played with a smooth and fluid motion. For now, play these on the snare drum. **Repeat each exercise several minutes without stopping.**

1. SINGLE STROKES (Leading with the RH)

2. SINGLE STROKES (Leading with the LH)

3. DOUBLE STROKES (Leading with the RH)   *Double strokes* consist of two consecutive strokes on each hand. Make each stroke steady and precise.

4. DOUBLE STROKES (Leading with the LH)

5. PARADIDDLES   A *paradiddle* is a combination of single strokes and double strokes. Watch the sticking closely as you play.

As stated earlier, these patterns are basic to drumming. You should practice them until the patterns are memorized and you can play them smoothly and reflexively. Later, you can practice them for speed.

Lesson 2:
Basic Reading

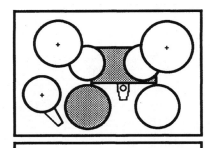

Basic Terms
Quarter Note & Rest
Half Note & Rest
Whole Note & Rest

In Lesson 1, we learned that the note most often thought of as one beat is the quarter note:

In music, notes are organized in groups called **measures.** Measures are formed by vertical lines called **bar lines.** Look at Exercise 1 on the following page, and you will notice that each measure has exactly four beats. The amount of beats (or counts) to each measure is determined by the stacked numbers you see at the beginning of the exercise:

= how many beats (counts) per measure
= indicates the quarter note receives one beat

This pair of numbers is called a **time signature.** The time signature always tells us how we are to count the music. Four/four time, which is the most commonly used time signature (most rock songs are in 4/4), simply means that there are four counts of quarter notes in each measure. Therefore, we will count each quarter note as we play it: "one, two, three, four, one, two," etc.

Note the double bar and dots at the end of Exercise 1:

This is called a **repeat sign.** A repeat sign directs us back to the beginning of the exercise, to play it once more.

As you play these exercises:

• Check for proper grip and position.
• Count the beats aloud as you play: 1,2,3,4,1,2,3,4, etc.
• Follow the indicated stickings. Alternating single strokes are to be used. Each exercise begins with the right stick, then alternates hand to hand.
• Make the notes even and precise. Keep the beat steady.
• Play steady quarter notes on the bass drum as you play the exercises. The bass drum is notated on the first space of the staff:

Bass Drum →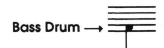

1.

Count:	1	2	3	4	1	2	3	4	1	2	3	4	1	2	3	4
Play:	R	L	R	L	R	L	R	L	R	L	R	L	R	L	R	L

QUARTER REST You already know that a quarter note indicates a beat (or count) to be played. A **quarter rest** indicates a beat (or count) not played. A quarter rest has exactly the same time value as a quarter note, so this rest must be counted, even though it is not played.

2.

Count:	1	2	3	4	1	2	3	4	1	2	3	4	1	2	3	4
Play:	R	L	R	–	R	L	R	–	R	L	R	–	R	L	R	–

3.

Count:	1	2	3	4	1	2	3	4	1	2	3	4	1	2	3	4
Play:	–	L	R	L	–	L	R	L	–	L	R	L	–	L	R	L

HALF NOTE The **half note** is always twice as long as a quarter note. In 4/4 time, since a quarter note equals one beat, a half note is two beats long. Think of it as one note that lasts for two counts. Strike the half note once, but give it two beats.

4.

Count:	1	2	3	4	1	2	3	4	1	2	3	4	1	2	3	4
Play:	R		L		R	L	R	L	R		L		R	L	R	L

HALF REST Every type of note has a corresponding rest, which has the **same value** as that note. The **half rest,** like the half note, is also equal to two beats (in 4/4 time); but two beats you count, and do not play.

5.

Count:	1	2	3	4	1	2	3	4	1	2	3	4	1	2	3	4
Play:	R	L	–	–	R	L	–	–	R	L	R	L	R	L	–	–

WHOLE NOTE 𝅝 The **whole note** is always twice as long as a half note. In 4/4 time, since the half note is two beats long, the whole note is four beats long. Strike the drum once, but give it four counts.

6. Count: 1 2 3 4 1 2 3 4 1 2 3 4 1 2 3 4
    Play: R – – – L R L R L – – – R L R L

WHOLE REST ▬ Like the quarter and half notes, the whole note also has a corresponding rest. In 4/4 time, the **whole rest** occupies an entire measure. The whole rest, like the whole note, is equal to four beats; but four beats you count, but do not play.

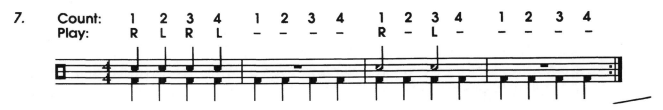

7. Count: 1 2 3 4 1 2 3 4 1 2 3 4 1 2 3 4
    Play: R L R L – – – – R – L – – – – –

COMBINATION EXERCISE

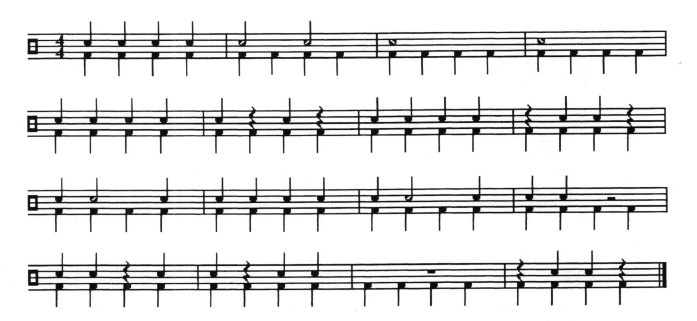

11

Lesson 3:
Eighth Notes

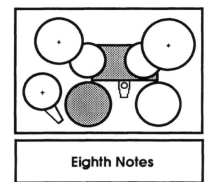

Eighth Notes

We now know three types of notes and their related rests: the whole note, the half note, and the quarter note. A good analogy for comparing the relationships of these three notes to each other is the measurement of an inch:

Think of a whole note as one inch:

Think of a half note as ½ of an inch:

Think of a quarter note as ¼ of an inch:

In a sense, notes are used to measure time (or duration) the same way inches are used to measure length. Just as a whole note can be broken down into two half notes, a half note can be broken down into two quarter notes, and a quarter note can be broken down into two eighth notes.

Eighth notes are exactly twice as fast as quarter notes.

The eighth note looks like a quarter note with a flag attached. When they are written consecutively, eighth notes can also be joined together by a **beam:**

Note the relationship of quarter notes to eighth notes:

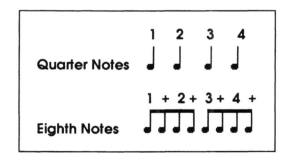

Note the indicated counting. We use the word "and" to account for the additional notes. The "ands" are to be played and counted **exactly** dead center between quarter notes. So, when eighth notes are to be played, we simply "double up" the beat. If quarter notes are one to the beat, eighth notes are two to the beat.

PREPARATORY EXERCISE   Look at this line. The first measure consists of quarter notes, while the second measure consists of eighth notes. The bass drum plays quarter notes throughout. You should practice this line repeatedly until you can easily feel the difference between quarter and eighth notes.

Now go on to the following exercises.

Lesson 4:
Eighth Rests

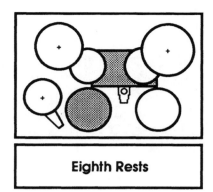

Eighth Rests

In this lesson, we will study the **eighth rest.** The eighth rest looks like this:

In previous lessons, you learned that every note has a corresponding rest with the same value. The eighth rest, therefore, has exactly the same value as the eighth note. It is important that you give the rests an equal amount of attention as you count these rhythms. Many drummers make the mistake of not paying enough attention to rests, and their reading suffers as a result. I advise you to count and "feel" the rests with the same intensity as you would count and "feel" the notes you play.

1.
Count: 1 + 2 3 4   1 + 2 3 4   1 + 2 3 4   1 2 3 4
Play: – R L R L   – R L R L   – R L R L   R L R L

2.
Count: 1 2 + 3 4   1 2 + 3 4   1 2 + 3 4   1 2 3 4
Play: R – L R L   R – L R L   R – L R L   R L R L

3.
Count: 1 2 3 + 4   1 2 3 + 4   1 2 3 + 4   1 2 3 4
Play: R L – R L   R L – R L   R L – R L   R L R L

4.
Count: 1 2 3 4 +   1 2 3 4 +   1 2 3 4 +   1 2 3 4
Play: R L R – L   R L R – L   R L R – L   R L R L

COMBINATION EXERCISE The following 32-measure study combines eighth notes and eighth rests. Make sure you can play this exercise accurately before you proceed.

Review Worksheet

Look at this chart and answer the following questions:

Whole Note	
Half Notes	
Quarter Notes	
Eighth Notes	

1. One whole note is equal to two _____ notes. One whole note is equal to ____ (how many) quarter notes.

2. One half note is equal to ____ (how many) quarter notes.

3. The time signature 4/4 tells how many beats there are in each measure. In 4/4 time there are ____ (how many) beats to a measure.

4. Measures are created by vertical lines called bar lines. In the music below there are ____ (how many) measures.

5. Now copy the above line. Don't forget the time signature and bar lines:

6. You know three types of sticking patterns: single strokes, double strokes, and paradiddles. Identify these stickings:

RLRR LRLL   These are _____.

RLRL RLRL   These are _____.

RRLL RRLL   These are _____.

7. Draw a line from each rest to the proper corresponding note:

Lesson 5:
Eighth-Note Rock Beats

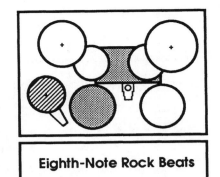

Eighth-Note Rock Beats

In this lesson you will be learning to play rock beats based on straight eighth notes. The most commonly used rock beats feature an *eighth-note ride pattern*. Play these eighth notes on the closed hi-hat, with your right hand crossing over. Play the snare drum part with your left hand, and of course the bass drum with your right foot. Align the bass drum and snare rhythm under the corresponding hi-hat note.

Here is the key to the notation used for this lesson:

Hi-Hat (RH) → ↓ ↓ ← **Open Hi-Hat**

← **Snare Drum (LH)**

Bass Drum (RF) → ■

In addition to the notation given for each beat, there is also a set of boxes for each beat, as a visual aid. Each box relates to one eighth-note count of the rock beat. On top of each box is the count for that part of the beat. Inside each box are abbreviations for which parts of the drum set are used for that particular count of the beat. The abbreviations used inside the boxes are:

HH   Hi-hat, to be played with the cymbals closed, with the right hand.
HH-o Hi-hat, to be played with the cymbals opened, with the right hand.
SN   Snare drum, to be played with the left hand.
BD   Bass drum, to be played with the right foot.

If you have trouble either reading the notation or coordinating your limbs, following the boxes should help. Play each box one by one, and go slowly enough to do them correctly. You can pick up the tempo once you are sure of yourself. Once you have the beat mastered, transfer your attention back to the notation. Keep the beat steady, smooth, and relaxed. Repeat each beat eight times.

Notation:

1.

Visual Key:

1	&	2	&	3	&	4	&
HH	HH	HH SN	HH	HH	HH	HH SN	HH
BD				BD			

2.

1	&	2	&	3	&	4	&
HH	HH	HH SN	HH	HH	HH	HH SN	HH
BD		BD	BD				

Notation:

Visual Key:

3.

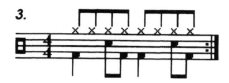

1	&	2	&	3	&	4	&
HH	HH	HH SN	HH	HH	HH	HH SN	HH
BD			BD	BD			BD

4.

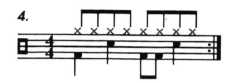

1	&	2	&	3	&	4	&
HH	HH	HH SN	HH	HH	HH	HH SN	HH
BD				BD	BD		

5.

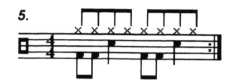

1	&	2	&	3	&	4	&
HH	HH	HH SN	HH	HH	HH	HH SN	HH
BD	BD			BD	BD		

6.

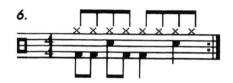

1	&	2	&	3	&	4	&
HH	HH	HH SN	HH	HH	HH	HH SN	HH
BD	BD		BD	BD			

7.

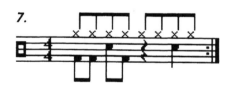

1	&	2	&	3	&	4	&
HH	HH	HH SN	HH	HH	HH	HH SN	HH
BD	BD		BD				

8.

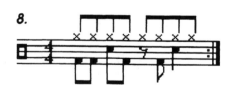

1	&	2	&	3	&	4	&
HH	HH	HH SN	HH	HH	HH	HH SN	HH
BD	BD		BD		BD		

9.

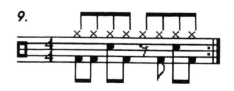

1	&	2	&	3	&	4	&
HH	HH	HH SN	HH	HH	HH	HH SN	HH
BD	BD		BD		BD		BD

10.

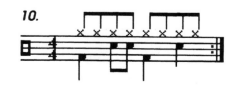

1	&	2	&	3	&	4	&
HH	HH	HH SN	HH SN	HH	HH	HH SN	HH
BD				BD			

Notation: **Visual Key:**

11.

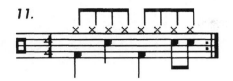

1	&	2	&	3	&	4	&
HH	HH	HH	HH	HH	HH	HH	HH
		SN				SN	SN
BD				BD			

12.

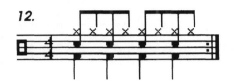

1	&	2	&	3	&	4	&
HH	HH	HH	HH	HH	HH	HH	HH
SN		SN		SN		SN	
BD		BD		BD		BD	

13.

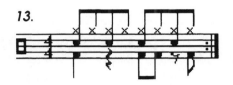

1	&	2	&	3	&	4	&
HH	HH	HH	HH	HH	HH	HH	HH
SN		SN		SN		SN	
BD				BD	BD		BD

14.

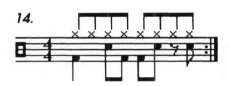

1	&	2	&	3	&	4	&
HH	HH	HH	HH	HH	HH	HH	HH
		SN			SN		SN
BD			BD	BD			

15.

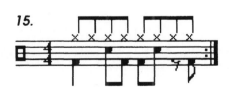

1	&	2	&	3	&	4	&
HH	HH	HH	HH	HH	HH	HH	HH
		SN			SN		
BD			BD	BD			BD

16.

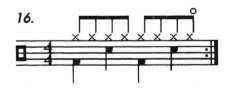

1	&	2	&	3	&	4	&
HH	HH	HH	HH	HH	HH	HH	HH-o
		SN				SN	
BD				BD			

17.

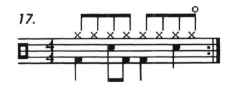

1	&	2	&	3	&	4	&
HH	HH	HH	HH	HH	HH	HH	HH-o
		SN				SN	
BD			BD	BD			

18.

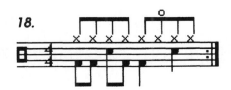

1	&	2	&	3	&	4	&
HH	HH	HH	HH	HH	HH-o	HH	HH
		SN				SN	
BD	BD		BD	BD			

21

Lesson 6:
Sixteenth Notes and Rests

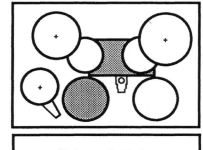

**Sixteenth Notes
Sixteenth Rests**

A quarter note can be broken down into two eighth notes:

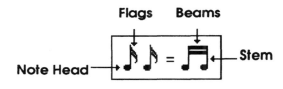

An eighth note can be broken down into two sixteenth notes:

When we play eighth notes in 4/4 time, we are playing "two to the beat" — we are dividing the quarter note into two equal parts. When we play sixteenth notes in 4/4 time, we are playing "four to the beat" — we are dividing the quarter note into four equal parts. Therefore, one quarter note is equal to four sixteenth notes. **Sixteenth notes are twice as fast as eighth notes.**

Single sixteenth notes have two flags connected to the stem. In groups, they are joined by two beams. And now is as good a time as any for you to know the parts of a note:

Sixteenth notes are counted as follows (use a long "e" and a short "a" to count "One-ee-and-ah, Two-ee-and-ah," etc.):

Practice playing and counting sixteenth notes against bass-drum quarter notes.

22

Now practice playing and counting the following exercise repeatedly, until the feel of sixteenth notes in relation to other notes is acquired. Keep your bass drum steady!

You are now ready to try the following exercises.

Sixteenth Rest

The **sixteenth rest** looks like this: $\boxed{\text{7}}$ It has the same time value as a sixteenth note. Like all rests, you should give it the same attention you would give a note. Count it, but do not play it. If the following exercises seem difficult, play them slowly at first.

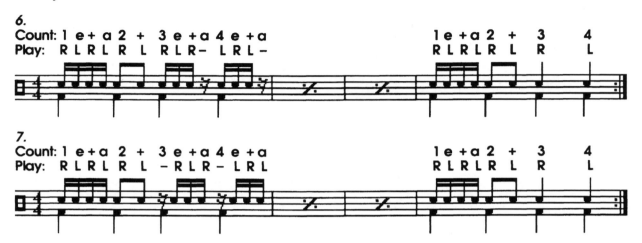

6.
Count: 1 e + a 2 + 3 e + a 4 e + a   1 e + a 2 + 3 4
Play: R L R L R L R L R– L R L–   R L R L R L R L

7.
Count: 1 e + a 2 + 3 e + a 4 e + a   1 e + a 2 + 3 4
Play: R L R L R L –R L R– L R L   R L R L R L R L

Lesson 7:
Two-Handed Sixteenth-Note Rock Beats

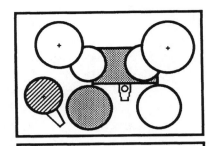

Two-Handed Sixteenth-Note Rock Beats

In this lesson, we will look at rock beats with a sixteenth-note ride pattern. Although sixteenth-note rock beats can be played with one hand on the hi-hat, they can also be played in a two-handed fashion: RLRL, RLRL, RLRL, RLRL, etc.

1. This beat has all the sixteenth notes played on the hi-hat.

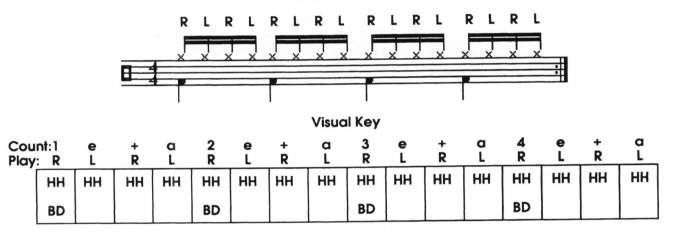

Visual Key

Count:	1	e	+	a	2	e	+	a	3	e	+	a	4	e	+	a
Play:	R	L	R	L	R	L	R	L	R	L	R	L	R	L	R	L
	HH	HH	HH	HH	HH	HH	HH	HH	HH	HH	HH	HH	HH	HH	HH	HH
	BD				BD				BD				BD			

2. This pattern has the backbeat on the snare, played with the **right stick**.

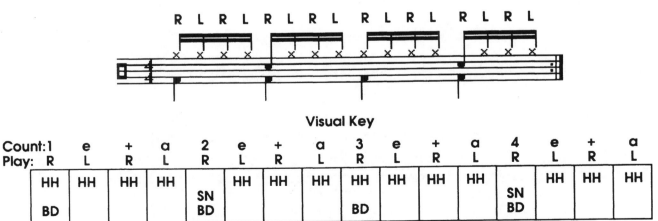

Visual Key

Count:	1	e	+	a	2	e	+	a	3	e	+	a	4	e	+	a
Play:	R	L	R	L	R	L	R	L	R	L	R	L	R	L	R	L
	HH	HH	HH	HH	SN	HH	HH	HH	HH	HH	HH	HH	SN	HH	HH	HH
	BD				BD				BD				BD			

3. This pattern is rhythmically the same as beat 2, the difference being the open hi-hats. When you realize that your feet are moving simultaneously here, it's not so hard to do.

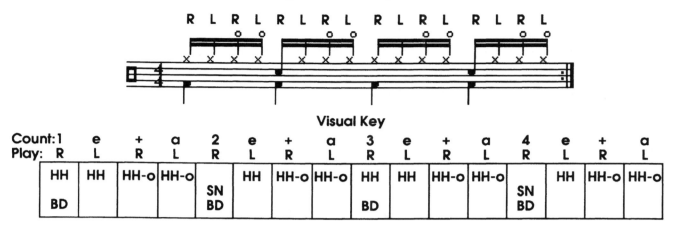

Visual Key

Count:	1	e	+	a	2	e	+	a	3	e	+	a	4	e	+	a
Play:	R	L	R	L	R	L	R	L	R	L	R	L	R	L	R	L
HH	HH	HH	HH-o	HH-o		HH	HH-o	HH-o	HH	HH	HH-o	HH-o		HH	HH-o	HH-o
	BD				SN / BD				BD				SN / BD			

4. In this situation, both hands are coming off the hi-hat at certain points to play the snare. Make sure there is plenty of room for your hands to maneuver around each other.

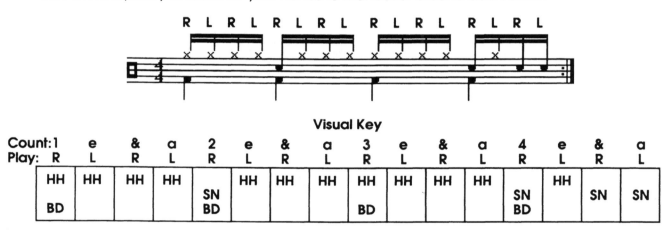

Visual Key

Count:	1	e	&	a	2	e	&	a	3	e	&	a	4	e	&	a
Play:	R	L	R	L	R	L	R	L	R	L	R	L	R	L	R	L
HH	HH	HH	HH	HH		HH	HH	HH	HH	HH	HH	HH		HH		
	BD				SN / BD				BD				SN / BD		SN	SN

5. This last sixteenth-note rock beat also utilizes both hands on the snare. It might be helpful to realize that, in all the above beats, there should be a steady, unbroken flow of sixteenth notes. Make sure your playing and counting are in sync.

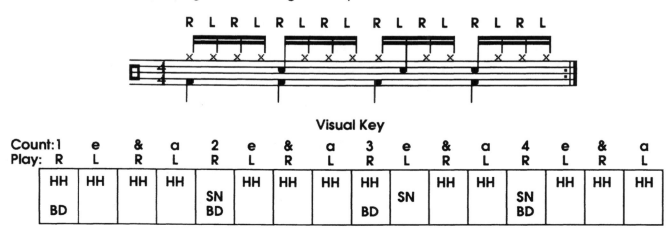

Visual Key

Count:	1	e	&	a	2	e	&	a	3	e	&	a	4	e	&	a
Play:	R	L	R	L	R	L	R	L	R	L	R	L	R	L	R	L
HH	HH	HH	HH	HH		HH	HH	HH	HH		HH	HH		HH	HH	HH
	BD				SN / BD				BD		SN		SN / BD			

Lesson 8:
Drum Fills

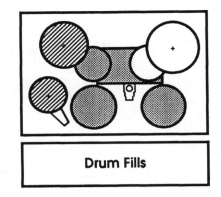

Drum Fills

What is a *drum fill*? A fill is a rhythmic figure the drummer plays as a change from the time-keeping pattern he had been maintaining. Although it is a small break in the pattern, the **tempo is not changed** at all, and in most instances the time-keeping pattern is resumed immediately after the fill. Fills can vary as to style, length, and dynamics. A fill can be soft and subtle, or loud and forceful. An important point to remember is that the flow of the music should not be sacrificed to the technicality of the fill. Actually, most fills are simple in structure and short in duration.

The fills in this lesson are based on this eighth-note rock beat:

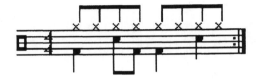

Note on the next page that each eighth-note rock beat is played three complete times, and that the fill occupies part (or all) of the fourth measure. These exercises are written this way for a reason. Most rock music (and most commercial music) is written in verses that are multiples of 4 in length. Therefore, it is important for a drummer to have a sense of what 4 measures "feels" like. If you can feel 4 measures, you can also feel 8, 12, 16, etc.

Fills are used for different reasons, the simplest being that they provide a break in the pattern being played. This break usually comes at the end of a 4-, 8-, 12-, 16-, or 32-measure section. Fills can also be transitional in nature. At the point where one section of a song runs into another (verse to chorus, verse to bridge, chorus to instrumental solo, etc.), a fill can be a useful pivotal point. Because fills can be a point of transition, they can also be considered musical "cues" to the listener that something new is coming up.

Legend of Notation: Two additions are made in our legend of notation. The high tom (usually mounted on the bass drum in front of the snare drum) and low tom (usually called a "floor tom" if it has legs; usually sits to the right of the snare drum):

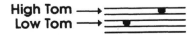

High Tom
Low Tom

27